T0343841

This book
belongs to:

_____

MADAME
Badobedah

For my adventurer crew: Jamie, Lyra and Moppy.
And to the Fiandacas, with whom we love a seaside adventure. — S. D.

For my mermaids — Fer, Madeleine and Yara.
With love and midnight swims. — L. O'H.

First published 2023 by Walker Books Ltd, 87 Vauxhall Walk, London SE11 5HJ

2 4 6 8 10 9 7 5 3 1

Text © 2023 Sophie Dahl • Illustrations © 2023 Lauren O'Hara
Hand lettering by Natalia O'Hara

The right of Sophie Dahl and Lauren O'Hara to be identified as author and illustrator respectively of this work has been asserted in accordance with the Copyright, Designs and Patents Act 1988

This book has been typeset in Joanna

Printed in China

British Library Cataloguing in Publication Data: a catalogue record for this book is available from the British Library

ISBN 978-1-4063-8442-0

www.walker.co.uk

SOPHIE DAHL

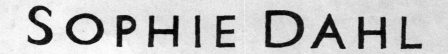

MADAME Badobedah

AND THE OLD BONES

illustrated by
LAUREN O'HARA

WALKER BOOKS
AND SUBSIDIARIES
LONDON · BOSTON · SYDNEY · AUCKLAND

Part One
The ancient villain

My name is Mabel,
and I'm an adventurer.

THE Mermaid Hotel

I live at The Mermaid Hotel, a place that's full to the brim with secrets.

My mum and dad are the managers. They look after the guests. My job is to keep an eye on them – you never know who could be staying.

Good grief, we've had ALL sorts.

A sailor with a trombone and pet ferret called Franco.

An opera-singing dame whose arias shook the ceilings.

A ballroom dancer with amber eyes and an identical twin.

A three-toed pygmy sloth, awfully fond of jam and gin.

And an ancient villain, with trunks of gold, accompanied

by dogs, cats AND the most suspicious-looking

tortoise I'd ever seen.

The ancient villain is our longest, oldest, best-ever guest. She's now officially a resident. She has eyes that smile, and toffee-apple hair. Her real name is Irena, but I call her Madame Badobedah. It rhymes with *ooooh la la*.

Madame Badobedah likes to eat sweets and build sandcastles. Many years ago, she was a ballet dancer in America, after she sailed across the sea, away from a war, to get there.

She has a teapot that wears a jumper. She can do a sort of creaky cartwheel.

Sometimes she is VERY rude to other grown-ups. But she's never rude to me.

Madame Badobedah has pirouetted
through pyramids, skated across rivers,
sailed with pirates, swum with mermaids,
and she may have once *borrowed*
Cleopatra's headdress.

These are the things I have done in my life
so far: steered a pirate ship away from perilous rocks
during a lashing storm AND learned my nine times table.

Before we were friends, I think Madame Badobedah
used to feel quite lonely. This made her cantankerous,
which is grown-up for very grumpy.

Now she is no longer growly, she mostly
says thank you and she sings when she
does the crossword.

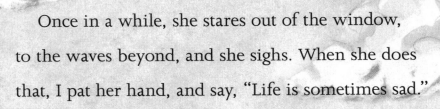

Once in a while, she stares out of the window,
to the waves beyond, and she sighs. When she does
that, I pat her hand, and say, "Life is sometimes sad."

She replies, "Yes, my *darlink* Mabel, it truly can be.
But sometimes it can be an absolute GLORY. And this
we must remember: the bothness of life, the sadness
and the glory.

"Now, shall we dance?"

And away we fly.

Part Two
Larking

On Saturdays,

if the weather is not too ferocious,

we will try our luck larking on the beach or

by the river. We're in the business of adventuring.

Hundreds of years ago, children searched the mud of the

river Thames, to see what the tides delivered. They were the

first larkers. It's like a lucky dip: you never know what will

turn up; you just need to have sharp eyes and patience.

Which I do and don't.

These are some things
we have found on our beach trips:

a type of shell that I call elephant's toenails, cloudy glass,
washed smooth by the sea, a message in a bottle, a mermaid's
violin, wishing stones (round stones with a hole in the
middle), pipes, beads.

Old sandwiches.

Here are things we haven't found yet:

a chest full of gold,

my headmaster, floating on a flamingo.

This Saturday, we waved to my mum, along with Beryl In Peril above the door. The wild winter wind greeted us like a friend.

Between October and May, Madame Badobedah wears about sixteen pairs of long johns and three coats and seven shawls and sometimes she looks like an enormous colourful ostrich with a hot-water bottle in her pocket.

"Oh, *darlink*, this is blowing all my cobwebs away!" Madame Badobedah laughed, her eyes glittering. "It certainly feels like a day for treasure; I can feel it in my waters."

"I can feel it in my waters, too!" I said. "I'd like to find an ammonite. Or a dinosaur. A Triceratops, I think."

"Old bones?" she replied, shaking her head. "I know a thing or two about them. What about a lovely sparkler instead? An emerald or a ruby? A sapphire?" she added hopefully.

"No. Dinosaurs are better. And ammonites are the jewels of the mollusc world, actually," I told her. "They were a sort of massive squid with a snail shell. Way better than a diamond!"

"I beg to differ," Madame Badobedah laughed. "Unless it's a squid-snail wearing a tiara. Then I might agree, Mabel dear."

15

We walked down the shingle path, hand
in hand, the stones crunching under our feet,
that friendly salt smell all around us. Madame
Badobedah swung her big handbag, which
could hold a small country.

On the beach, we got to looking. In the
beginning, it was the usual stuff, an old crab
shell, a bit of wood with barnacles, cuttlefish, and
ropes and ropes of seaweed. Nestled in its lacy
folds, I saw something round and glinting gold.

It was a coin. I picked it up and rubbed the sand gently off with my shirt. I'd never seen one like it; it had the face of a man who looked like a kindly pufferfish, wearing leaves on his head instead of a crown.

"Well, there you are." Madame Badobedah smiled. "Those sharp eyes are working, Miss Mabel. Just think of who could have held that before you, what a life it has lived, this little coin."

And I thought about that for a bit, because I like thinking about the stories of things, and how they came to be.

"Why don't you make a wish?" Madame Badobedah said. "That's the thing to do with a lucky coin."

I screwed up my eyes and thought of all the things in the world that were waiting to be discovered, or re-discovered, in the earth, below, above and to the side of us.

"I wish for a big adventure,"

I whispered.

Part Three

The dressing table of dreams

The next day was Sunday, and on
Sundays Madame Badobedah and I
meet in Room 32 for elevenses,

which is somewhere between breakfast

and lunch and has a biscuit.

Room 32 is the best room in the hotel because it
contains Madame Badobedah, two dogs, two cats, a
tortoise, a magic cupboard AND Madame Badobedah's
dressing table, which has about 507 drawers. It could
be 570. I started counting them once but there were so
many I lost track halfway through.

"Throw those curtains wide, *darlink*!" Madame
Badobedah laughed. "It's time to see what's in the
dressing table of dreams. Pick a drawer, any drawer."

"Hmm. Drawer 503, please," I said.

Madame Badobedah stood theatrically next to the dressing table, and peered at the drawers.

"Now, is this 503? No, that's 436. We won't look in there; I think there's an old mummy's curse from Egypt rattling about in that one. 208 has a similar situation: a banshee, last seen causing lots of trouble around a bog in County Kerry. A drawer is the best place for her, poor *darlink* – she's a shrieker. And 105 – well, we won't get into that, but the Lady of the Lake most CERTAINLY didn't need that sword any more."

"I think this is it," she said, pulling open a drawer near the bottom. A shimmering green light filled the room. "Oh, heavens above," Madame Badobedah groaned and slammed it shut.

"What the dickens is that?" I asked.

"*Darlink*, it's nothing. I'd totally forgotten I had it. It's not even the right drawer."

"Shady," I said. "DEEPLY suspicious, in fact."

"We'll come back to it, Mabel. Ah ha, drawer 503. Thank you, dear dressing table! Now, this is fascinating…" Out came her hand, brandishing an enormous, grubby FANG.

"Well, that didn't belong to a tooth-brusher," I said. "Whose was it?"

"Come and sit on the pirate ship, and I'll tell you."

I sat on her bed, where Madame Badobedah took a sip of tea and began.

"Long ago, after I was a ballet dancer, and before I made dresses, I was an explorer.

"I was one of the first in a long tradition of adventurers: Mary Anning, Zora Neale Hurston and Amelia Earhart among them. We should know the names of these brave pioneers, Mabel!

Zora Neale Hurston

Mary Anning

Amelia Earhart

"I was leading an expedition in North America, having been told of a rare medicinal plant that could be found there…"

The pirate ship became surrounded by tall trees, and the smell of pine. Water dripped on my nose.

Madame Badobedah continued. "And after many days, I finally located the darn thing. I was heading back to base, with it safely in my handbag. Fern fronds were tickling my nose, it was raining, cats and dogs, *darlink*, when I heard a thunderous noise. This noise was accompanied by an echoing groan.

"In a clearing, I came upon the most fantastic beast, with three horns and a frill around his neck, making a frightful racket."

"Three horns?!" I said.

"Yes, Mabel, as you might be guessing, it was a Triceratops. A Triceratops with the most awful toothache, poor fellow."

"IMPOSSIBLE!" I shouted.

"*Darlink*, I told you, I am absolutely prehistoric; this should come as no surprise. And nothing is impossible. Not only did I meet him; I got rid of his toothache.

"He was bellowing, and thrashing around, and so I sat next to him.

"Sometimes creatures, animals and humans, just need someone to sit with them, to know that they're not alone.

We looked at each other in the eye. I could see he was in great pain. In my marvellous handbag, I had the juice of the plant that I earlier extracted, and some twine. I knew what to do. I asked him permission – with my eyes – I reached into his great mouth, and could see that offending tooth a mile off. I tied the twine around it and gave it a YANK, and, boom, out it came. He was so surprised he sat down next to me. I rubbed the medicine on his gum.

"'Bravo, sir. Well done, you,' I told him. 'You were splendidly brave.' And after that, he let me give him a pat and off I went."

My mouth was open. "Did you TRULY meet a Triceratops?" I asked her.

"Oh, certainly I did," Madame Badobedah said breezily, as she stroked her dogs. "I've done a lot of things, let me tell you.

"Now, you probably know this already, Mabel, because you're the cleverest person I know, but Triceratops could have up to eight hundred teeth. One of them gone isn't much of a problem. But the … AHEM … the ITEM, in the other drawer – well, that's a bit more troublesome. I *borrowed* it some years ago and always meant to return it. The time is ripe. I'll meet you after you've had dinner.

Mermaid Cupboard. Wear your best spy costume.

We'll be going incognito."

Part Four

Old bones

Madame Badobedah answered
the door in a black velvet catsuit.

A bulging pouch hung from her neck, its green

light radiating on her face. Nervously,

she scanned the corridor.

"Excellent costume, Captain." She nodded her approval. "Shall we?" She ushered me in.

There were butterflies pirouetting around my stomach, and I rubbed my lucky coin.

We crawled past her dresses and spiky shoes, to the very back of the cupboard. It smelled like her, of roses and vanilla. The green glow around her neck lit the way.

It was me who first showed Madame Badobedah the secret of Room 32, when she said sorry and meant it, and I knew we could be friends.

"Now, *darlink*, you know the drill," she said. "It's your cupboard. Your magic." I held her hand and knocked on the last rafter three times. I squeezed the coin and shut my eyes.

When I opened them, a blast of cold air hit my face. We stood outside a huge, gothic building, in the dark. Snow dusted the ground.

The Natural History Museum, a sign read.

"Well, this is VERY UNUSUAL," I said to Madame Badobedah, raising one eyebrow.

She looked a bit suspicious, the sneaky ostrich.

"Toffee, *darlink?*" she offered. "I find they always help me think so much better. It's the chewing, you see." I took a toffee and squinted at her.

"Why are we here when it's shut?" I asked. "Who's going to let us in?"

"Well, it's just an unofficial visit to return something I borrowed when I was here years ago, giving a talk about explorers. On a trip to the loo, I happened to spot a sparkler that was calling my name, and I popped it in my pocket for safekeeping. Oh, I adore emeralds, Mabel."

"Madame Badobedah!" I said sternly. "Do you mean to tell me you have a precious jewel from the Natural History Museum on your person, at this very moment? That you've had it for years?!"

She winked. "Darlink, the less said, the better. It was in

36

the cellar, though, poor emerald, not getting any love. And, whether you're judging me or not, which you shouldn't, because people are complicated, this is the PERFECT Sunday night outing."

We climbed the stone steps, melting into the shadows. My heart was thudding. I saw her veined hands reach for the door, and I don't know what sorcery she did, but it opened, with an echo.

"Like butter," Madame Badobedah said, chuckling. "Oh ho, there's life in this old girl yet, Mabel!"

We stood together, in the great cathedral of a hall in the Natural History Museum, and we breathed it in. I looked up.

"A massive whale is watching us," I whispered.

"So it is," Madame Badobedah said. "Nosy parker! Now, I must make my delivery. And you, my *darlink*, have a look: there's much for an adventurer to find here. Back in a tick."

Footsteps always sound louder in the dark, if you're out of bed, or somewhere you shouldn't be. Creak, creak, thud. I could hear Madame Badobedah's knees joining in, like the joists of an ancient ship, as she walked away.

The skeletons of an Iguanodon, T. rex and Triceratops regarded me coolly.

"Um, hello," I said, feeling a bit embarrassed. "Sorry to drop in uninvited. I'm Mabel. I think I might like to be a palaeontologist when I'm older. I wish we could have met when you were alive. Iguanodon, I would have fed you some leaves. T. rex, you'd probably have eaten me. And, Triceratops, we could've talked, but I think you were shy – a bit of a loner. Like Madame Badobedah used to be. She's my best friend, although I think she might be about to get us arrested."

"Madame Badobedah, did you say?" a voice boomed. "Be still, my beating heart. How divine!"

I thought I might faint.

A Triceratops was talking to me

in the velvet darkness. "She pulled out my

troublesome tooth, way back when," the dinosaur said.

"Oh, what a woman! T. rex, Iguanodon, you must meet her."

    "I take offence to the suggestion I would have eaten you,

young woman." T. rex grinned, teeth gleaming. "I wouldn't.

I'm practically vegetarian. Perhaps the occasional Triceratops,

as a treat. Juicy and the right amount of spiky."

    "Steady on," Triceratops said to him, crossly.

    "I didn't mean to offend you," I said. I addressed

the three of them. "I didn't think you'd

actually answer, you see."

    Triceratops smiled down at me.

"Why wouldn't we, my dear girl?

You called."

Creak, creak, thud. Madame Badobedah had returned. The pouch around her neck was now gone. She was full of glee as she waved at the Triceratops.

"My dear old friend, how are you? Teeth are looking marvellous!"

"Madame!" he said and bowed his head. The other dinosaurs followed suit.

Madame Badobedah winked, and patted T. rex, who purred like a kitten.

"*Darlinks*, I see you've met my dear Mabel," she said. "A dinosaur enthusiast extraordinaire."

"We're huge fans," Triceratops pronounced. "She's interested and curious. And, like your good self, an adventurer."

"She is," Madame Badobedah said. "She's all those things, and much, much more."

She held my gaze and sighed.

"My dears, I fear we cannot stay. I may have set off an invisible alarm system, as sadly my flexibility is not as it once was. And, Mabel, I so wanted to show you the coprolites. Alas, it's time to bid these bones adieu."

I looked at her, questioningly.

"It means goodbye," she said. "NOW."

"Byeeeeeee!" I sang, my voice echoing through that enormous room.

And oh, my days, we ran.

Room 32 was warm and cosy, exactly as we left it, our racing hearts and frosty fingers the only clues as to where we'd been.

Madame Badobedah says that we are all connected to the past by invisible threads we can't see, but that we can touch.

"When you hold your coin, Mabel, think about the other adventurers who've held it, over hundreds of years, and what they've dreamed of and wished for. All these centuries on, different people, but so many of our wishes are still the same."

She smiled her big smile at me, and her green eyes shone. "It makes me feel like I'm a part of a huge, ancient family, *darlink*. I find it very reassuring."

Madame Badobedah squeezed my hand. In the other,
I held my coin and the tooth of an ancient talking
dinosaur. Outside the window of The Mermaid Hotel,
the sea sang its song and snow began to fall.

A long time ago, the pilot Amelia Earhart said,
"Adventure is worthwhile in itself." She was right. I know
that there are untold worlds to discover if we just
keep our eyes sharp, and our hearts open.
I'm ready.

The End